LITTLE BLACK BOOK OF SAFETY

SAFETY GUIDE FOR RIDESHARE DRIVERS

BY

KEISHA GEBRE

$\mathcal{F}$or years taxi/ rideshare drivers have led the

list of;

" What professions you are most likely to be murdered?"

Although there has been a slight decline in the murder rate over the years, unfortunately, taxi/rideshare drivers remain on the deadliest job list, according to the United States Bureau of labor. The Bureau conducted a census of Fatal Occupational Injuries, and the results concluded that about 17 taxi/rideshare drivers are murdered per 100,000 workers. This murder rate almost doubles that of police officers. Taxi/rideshare drivers also have a homicide rate over 20 times that of the average worker.

Taxi/rideshare drivers often work odd hours and are an easy target for dangerous individuals.

While seasoned taxi drivers know the inns and out of the industry and go through extensive safety training, which helps them spot a potential attacker, most rideshare drivers, unfortunately, don't come into the profession with the same amount of training or experience. Because of its flexible scheduling, not having a "real boss," and secure payment and fare structure, rideshare driving has become the ultimate side hustle for many professionals looking to make some extra cash alongside their full-time job.

Below you will find the demographic of the average rideshare driver.

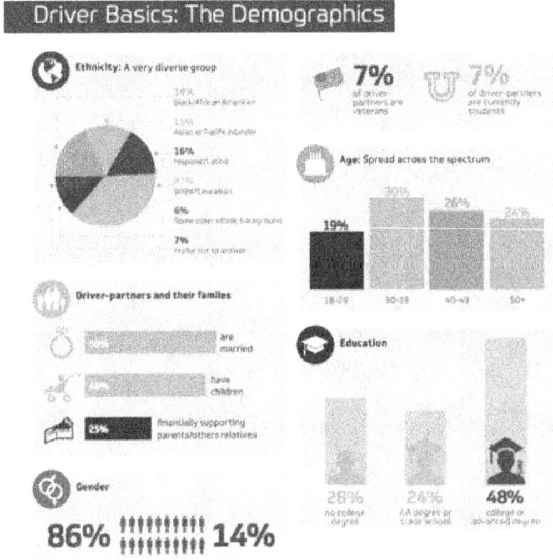

Image credit: Uber

This book was designed to be a basic safety guide for rideshare drivers. It contains basic safety practices and procedures that should evaluate risks or potential risks of harm and how to respond to those risks based on standard safety procedure guidelines.

The book is divided into nine main sections. These include;

1. Self-defense tools .
2. Analysis of passengers.
3. What pre-attack indicators to look for?
4. What to do if carjacked and or Robbed?
5. What to do if Kidnapped?
6. What procedures may be employed to make it out alive of a kidnapping?
7. Medical Attention.
8. The rescue.
9. Additional Information.

SELF DEFENSE TOOLS

Although most rideshare services come with state-of-the-art technology that can track every trip, you still need to prepare your vehicle for any unfortunate eventualities.

Here are a few things to consider having in your vehicle before picking up passengers:

This is an exhaustive list. Choose the self-defense tool you are more comfortable using and that you think is more applicable to your route, State, Country, or situation.

Dashcam

If you are a rideshare driver, having a dashcam is a must. Not only will it serve as evidence if you are involved in an accident, but it will also allow you to monitor what your passengers are doing in your vehicle.

As a driver, your primary concern should be how you can protect yourself and your passengers if things don't go as expected.

For example, you may have a passenger who physically or verbally assaults you.

Having a dashcam will not only act as a way for you to prove that the incident occurred and give relevant details, but it will also deter others. When someone knows that they are being watched, they tend to behave better.

- If a passenger makes a false claim against you, your dashcam will assist in providing evidence that you were following the rules laid down by your company.
- In the unfortunate event that a passenger attempts to rob, kidnap or carjack you, you can quickly employ emergency procedures that may save your life by monitoring your dashcam. The video footage will also provide valuable information to investigators if you are victimized and or kidnapped.

There are many dashcams on the market now; shop around for the best one for you. It's my recommendation that you look for a dashcam devise that has more than one camera (2 or 3 cameras) that can record what happens both inside and outside the car simultaneously.

Portable Taxi Window

Portable taxi windows are great for shielding yourself from passengers. They provide a partisan that divides the front seat from the backseat.

Most are easy to install. They can be put in place quickly and taken down and stored when not use

These devices serve a dual purpose:

1. They act as a sneeze guard, which gives added protection from exposure to respiratory droplets.

2. They provide a physical barrier in the vehicle, which will give you time to escape or prepare for an attack.

Due to the COVID pandemic, there is a wide variety from which to choose.

However, I do recommend that you look for one with a hard acrylic resin finish. Prices typically range between USD 35.00 to $150.00. Partisans with more advanced features will cost more.

Taser (if legal in your State or Country)

These devices work by delivering a high voltage, low -current electrical discharge into the body of an attacker, overwhelming the muscle- triggering mechanisms of their body. The shock is painful and can temporarily paralyze the attacker. Tasers differ from stun guns because stun guns require direct contact with the attacker, while tasers can be used up to 15 feet away or more. I recommend tasers but choose the one you feel more comfortable using. In an emergency, you might not be able to decide where to aim but try, if it's possible, to aim at the torso or any area from the hips to the lower neck. Avoid, if possible, any area covered with clothes: Your attacker will most likely be attacking from behind, so try to aim for the neck or chest area; once the attacker is incapacitated, run as quickly as you can to safety.

It is essential to mention that things happen within a matter of seconds when attacked. Regular practice with your taser is critical, as this will ensure that you have the skill and confidence to use it in an emergency. Additionally, muscle memory is invaluable when defending yourself.

Please do not practice on a human or animal. Find objects of varying heights and sizes. Try to recreate different scenarios of being attacked in your vehicle and how you will respond with your taser if this occurs.

Licensed firearm (if legal in your State or Country)

Many States and Countries have passed laws permitting citizens to carry concealed handguns. There is also a continuing strengthening of laws allowing the use of deadly force in self-defense.

It is imperative to check the law in your State and or Country, as well as the rideshare company you are attached to if it is permissible for you to carry a concealed handgun.

Deciding to arm yourself is a decision that should be carefully and thoroughly considered. Special attention needs to be placed on the required training and the legal aftermath if you are ever put in a position to use the handgun.

Some States or Countries have outlawed the use of certain types of guns, such as guns with silencers and automatic weapons, etc. If you would like to carry a gun to protect yourself while working, you should choose a legal weapon in your State or Country. You should also check whether your State or Country permits "concealed carry" and whether you need a permit or license.

Using a gun for self-defense should be a last resort. It should not be used to resolve petty arguments or incidents. It should only be used if you find that your life is in imminent and immediate danger.

Pepper Spray

The active ingredient in pepper spray is capsicum peppers. These peppers go through a finely grounded process, from which the capsicum is extracted. It is then mixed with an organic solvent like ethanol.

These compact little devices come in a wide variety of sizes, shapes, colors, and designs.

Manufacturers have become extremely creative over the years and have cleverly designed canisters that can easily be hidden in clear view. They can be attached to your keys, tucked in your pocket, purse, compartment by your car door, or placed between your legs as you drive.

However, you need to ensure that your pepper spray canister is easily accessible from wherever you decide to keep it.

Made to cause facial irritation, spray up and down an attacker's face for optimal effect. Yell throughout the attack. This will not only increase the feeling of confusion but will also draw much-needed attention. Once the spray takes effect, run as fast as possible to safety.

Mace

Mace contains a unique formulation of tear gas and pepper solution in a solvent blend with dry nitrogen as a propellant. These ingredients produce a strong and effective humane deterrent for protection against an attack. Point and spray short bursts at the facial area off the attacker. Direct eye or nasal contact will be more effective, but anywhere you can aim at the face will cause discomfort to your attacker. All you need is a couple of seconds for you to escape.

It is important to cover your nose, keep your mouth closed and have your door slightly jarred

or window down if possible before and during
use.

Tactical Flashlight

Tactical flashlights were initially designed and manufactured to be used in conjunction with a firearm. Their primary purpose was to assist with target identification in areas where there is limited lighting. Rather than wielding a separate flashlight, it would allow a marksman (law enforcement, security, or military) to aim a weapon and illuminate a target at the same time.

Over the years, these flashlights have been re-engineered and redesigned as a stand-alone flashlight, which the general population can now use. They make great self-defense weapons, especially for rideshare drivers. Here are a few reasons:

- o They tend to be smaller than traditional flashlights, which means they can be easily concealed in your pocket, on your belt in a unique holster, or under or between your legs as you drive.

- o They emit much more light than traditional flashlights, with most putting out a setting of about 300 lumens of light, which, if pointed directly at the eyes, is more than enough to blind or disorient a potential attacker temporarily. Since the blindness is temporary, this will buy you a couple of seconds to either escape, strike the attacker with the flashlight or use another self-defense weapon. It is my recommendation that you purchase one that has a strobe setting. Immediately after temporarily blinding your attacker, he/she will likely try to cover their face with their hands. By activating the strobe setting, this will help enhance your attacker's feeling of disorientation, giving you a few more valuable additional seconds.

o   Most tactical flashlights are made of weapon-grade aluminum, and some also have a serrated or toothed bezel. These flashlights were purposefully manufactured and designed with this material, so they can also be used to deliver a deadly blow to your attacker.

Baton

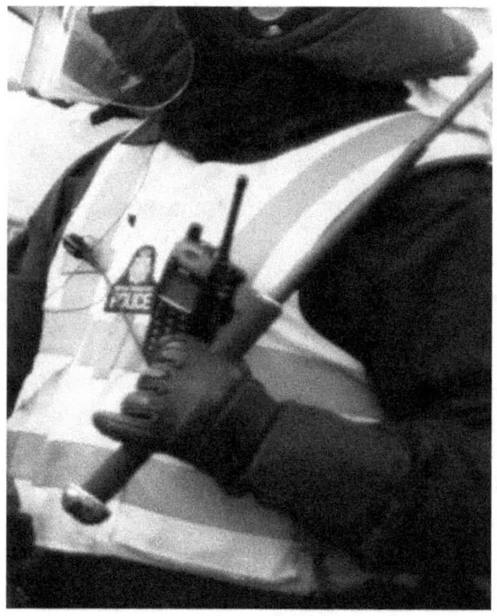

Batons are great self-defense tools for rideshare drivers as they are easy to swing and wield and require no prior training.

They are generally legal to own in most States or Countries; however, there are a few States or Countries where civilians without a valid permit cannot use Batons for self-defense purposes. I strongly recommend that you check your State or

Country's laws before considering purchasing this self-defense tool.

As I stated earlier, Batons are great for self-defense. They are much easier to use than a knife, gun, or taser. They are also easy to conceal as they can be placed under your car's seat and pulled out quickly if needed.

Because you will probably be sitting if attacked, you will need to aim for your attacker's head or face. Aim for the temple, nose, eyes, or the back of the head where the spine meets the base of the skull. These are all very vulnerable areas that will incapacitate your attacker, allowing you an opportunity to escape.

If using this self-defense tool, you must be prepared to strike and to strike hard. Give full hard swings and swing all the way through, back and forth. A halfhearted approach can backfire, putting you in an unsafe situation.

There have been instances where assailants have wrestled the victim, taken the baton, and then turned around and used it on the victim. To minimize this from happening, I recommend that you get an expandable baton. These batons are usually made from steel, which can expand and detract. The tips are much smaller, making it more difficult for the assailant to grab and hold.

Whichever baton you chose to purchase, your attacker's probability of grabbing the baton must be kept in mind.

If this happens, place both hands firmly on the baton and create fast and hard circles to break the attacker's grip, then immediately pull the baton to you.

Tactical Knife

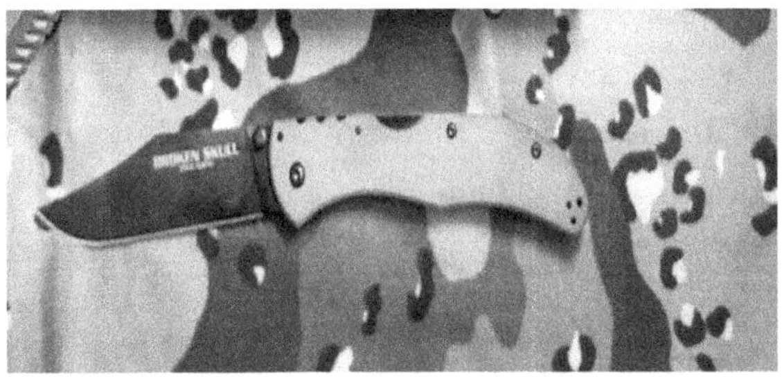

Tactical knives are usually small and relatively easy to conceal, making them an excellent self-defense tool for rideshare drivers.

Some States and or Countries have laws against blades that are a certain length, and they also have specific regulations on the use of switchblades versus folding knives. I recommend that you check the relevant laws that govern where you reside. I also recommend that you check with your company if carrying a knife of any kind is permissible.

If you chose to use this self-defense tool, it would be best to place it somewhere that is safe and won't cause you injury and that you can access quickly and easily if needed.

There are different tactical knives on the market; they come in many different shapes that can be used to perform various motions. Only you can decide how much damage you would like to inflict on a would-be attacker, but please remember that this weapon can be lethal, so you must mentally prepare yourself before use.

Whichever tactical knife you decide to purchase is entirely up to you. However, I recommend that you choose one with a durable blade that won't break in the heat of a battle.

If you don't have any prior experience using a tactical knife, it is essential to practice at home. Knowing how to open the knife quickly and where to aim is necessary as an attacker can wrestle it out of your hands and use it against you.

You will probably be sitting if attacked, so aim anywhere on the upper body that is within reach. While stabbing certain areas can be deadly, stabbing other regions will only inflict pain and not necessarily incapacitate your attacker. The intensity of the situation may not allow you to examine where you have stabbed the attacker, so it is my recommendation that you run as quickly as you can to safety after use.

Tactical Pen

Tactical pens are not as effective at causing injury to an attacker as tactical knives. Still, they serve as a great backup and, if used correctly, can buy you a couple of seconds so that you can distance yourself and escape a dangerous situation.

They are also legal to carry in most States or Countries, but I recommend checking the laws where you reside to make sure.

Designed to look like an actual pen, these devices are easy to conceal and great for surprise attacks. Some are made from incredibly durable weapon-grade material so you can strike an attacker and cause a bit of damage.

It is essential to mention that it will be challenging to incapacitate an attacker with a tactical pen, so it is crucial to have a plan B after use.

Tactical Rings

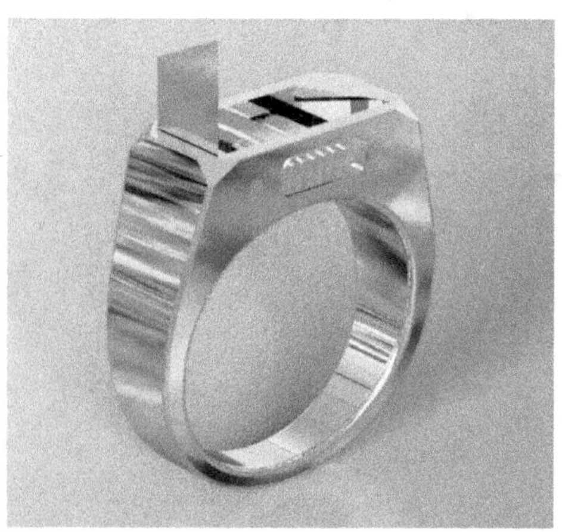

These are great for rideshare drivers as they are easy to conceal and legal to wear in almost every State and or Country. (I still recommend that you check your local laws to be extra sure).

Designed to look like a piece of jewelry, these rings are excellent for surprise attacks. They have a hidden shim pick made from weapon-grade steel that, if used correctly, can stab and stun your attacker, giving you precious seconds so that you can escape a dangerous situation.

It is important to mention that the pick on a tactical ring is short and will not incapacitate your attacker, so if using this self-defense weapon, be sure to have a backup or a plan B.

Schrill Alarm

Schrill alarms are great safety devices for rideshare drivers. These small little pocket alarms are made up of compressed air or gas. They emit a shrill piercing and deafening 110 dB high-frequency tone that will not only surprise and scare a would-be attacker, but the sound is almost unbearable, so it's practically guaranteed that they will immediately try to cover their ears, giving you enough time to grab another self-defense tool and or quickly escape. Because of the size, they are easy to stick in your purse, pocket, or glove compartment of your car. They do not require any batteries, and the device is easy to activate even in panic situations. However, I do recommend that you read the manual for instructions on how to use it correctly.

Please do not wait until you're in an emergency to try to figure out how it works; get familiar with the device the minute purchased. Not knowing what to do will cost you valuable seconds, which could mean the difference between life or death.

ANALYZING PASSENGERS

-
-

Now that you have prepared your vehicle for all eventualities, you now need to mentally prepare yourself to analyze your passenger. I recommend that you make it a habit of conducting a mini risk assessment of each passenger and the environment each time you respond to a booking.

Your risk analysis of your passenger and the surroundings should begin the minute you approach the pick-up location.

Here are a few things to consider:

- Immediately identify your emergency escape route.
- Try to stop somewhere that you cannot be blocked in.

- Never drive into alleys, paths, trails, or back lanes. Advise passengers that it is company policy, and you are not allowed to do that. Alleys, paths, trails, and back lanes are prime locations for homicides.

- Avoid driving into private gated homes. Ask passengers to meet you outside on the main road.

- If driving into a gated community, drive around and find the closet exit before stopping to pick up your passenger.

- If you pick up your passengers at night, stop in a well-lit spot, preferably one where there are lots of people and where you can see, and your visibility is high.

- Keep your windows rolled up and your doors locked. Only unlock the doors when you feel comfortable doing so.

- After seeing your passenger or passengers, follow your gut instinct; if you have an uncomfortable feeling, drive off, it is better to lose a few dollars than it is to lose your life, remember you can always get another passenger.

- Carefully scan your surroundings, look around for any suspicious activity. Now is not the time to be distracted by other activities or on your phone.

- Examine your passenger as they walk to the vehicle. I recommend that if they have bags that you ask them to place them in the trunk. Your dashcam will come in handy at this point. Take a glance at your dashcam before getting out to assist. You need to do this for two main reasons; 1) observe the bag or bags and 2) watch your passenger's demeanor.

  If you choose to get out of your vehicle to assist, remember to have your keys either in your pocket or firmly in your hand while at the same time scanning for any unusual activity.

- Pay special attention to your passengers' clothes; is there anything protruding or bulging from their bodies? This won't be easy to do if your passenger has on a coat or very big or roomy clothing, so you need to pay very close attention. Without being a fashion police, if you notice a sweater or jacket that doesn't fit with what the passenger is wearing or the season, this should ping your radar as this is a sign that they may be carrying a weapon. The same is true if the passenger comes out with an open jacket in inclement weather; this is also a sign that they may be carrying a weapon.

- Look at how they walk and how they enter the vehicle; if they have a gun, knife, or a blunt object, you will often find that they have a shortened stride and that they lean ever so slightly. This slight tilt of the body usually is done unconsciously as the mind knows that there is a presence of something strapped to the body that generally wouldn't be there. The tilt will be to whichever side of their body that has the dominant hand; a big clue to finding their dominant hand is whichever hand they have a wristwatch on, or they open the door or gate with. Most people will tilt to their right side as more than 90% of the population is right-handed, and this will be their stronger side and the side they are more comfortable performing tasks with. So, it will more likely be the side that they use to pull out the weapon.

- Observe if the passenger is touching or resting their hand on a particular area of their body as they walk or sit.
- Another indicator that your passenger may have a weapon is if one arm is rigid and stiff.
- If they have one hand gloved and the other in their pocket as they approach the vehicle, this is also an indicator that they may have a weapon.
- They may also not want to bend their knees to get in the vehicle if they have a weapon in their pants.

If you suspect that a passenger has a gun, I recommend that you drive off, don't let them get in the vehicle. If the passenger has already entered your car, immediately get out and get help. While the passenger may be just another concerned citizen, lawfully carrying a firearm for protection, the probability does exist that they may have ill intent. Remember, there are no do-overs when it comes to saving your life. It's better to be overly cautious.

- Be on the lookout for passengers who might have a drug addiction. If a passenger enters your vehicle and has any apparent signs of drug abuse, this should be considered a warning cue, and I do not recommend that you transport this passenger. If you decide to transport this passenger, please make sure to be on high alert and have your self-defense tools in place.

Signs to look for; the presence of lots of scabs on the skin, itching motions (crank bugs), bloodshot or glazed eyes, dilated or constricted pupils, needle tracks, muscle tics, and small bruises on the extremities are some indicators of drug use. While not all drug users are predatory criminals, many predatory criminals are drug users. Take the necessary precautions.

- If a passenger enters your vehicle and is intoxicated (alcohol or drugs) as a ride care driver, you automatically assume a duty of care for that passenger's safety until they arrive at their destination.

  Intoxicated passengers can be very unpredictable; some will sleep, some will talk, others will be overly friendly, and a few will be extremely aggressive and violent.

  I recommend that you ensure that your dashcam is turned on and recording. You can also record the ride with your cell phone for added protection. If anything happens that leads to a potential lawsuit, the footage from your dashcam and your cell phone video can both be used as evidence. I also recommend that you have your self-defense tools in place for easy access.

- If a passenger exhibits any sign of mental illness, please be on extremely high alert while transporting them.

Unlike many physical illnesses, mental illness isn't always visible, and most people aren't professionally diagnosed and don't even know they have a mental disorder.

Under the Americans with Disability Act, patients do not have to reveal that they have a mental illness.

However, you have to take the necessary precautions to safeguard yourself.

According to the American Psychiatric Association, there are a few indicators to look for; these include:

I. If a passenger looks anxious or worried.

II. If a passenger has an emotional outburst.

III. Vague look in their eyes while speaking to them, where you sense a disconnect from the conversation.

IV.   Has heightened sensitivity to sights, sounds, smells, or touch.

V.   Illogical thinking, where they are making statements about unusual or exaggerated personal beliefs.

VI.   A passenger exhibits peculiar behavior that you find odd or unusual.

While most people with mental illness aren't particularly violent, there have been a few instances where mentally ill individuals have attacked rideshare/taxi drivers.

- If transporting a single passenger, never let that passenger sit directly behind you. Statistics have revealed that more than 80% of all attacks on taxi/rideshare drivers are from passengers who were seated directly behind the driver. Be polite and use your creativity when finding an excuse to ask the passenger to move to the other side. Regularly monitor your dashcam while driving. This will allow you to know exactly what the passenger is doing, and it will also send a message to the passenger that you see them.

- Use your discernment when transporting three or more individuals. Immediately upon seeing your potential passengers conduct an impromptu risk assessment of each passenger. Pay special attention to their body language and clothing as they approach the vehicle. If you have an uncomfortable feeling, drive off. Remember, the more individuals that you have in your vehicle, the harder it will be to defend yourself if the need arises.

- Discourage passengers from sitting in the front seat; when a passenger is seated in the front seat, they can quickly launch a surprise attack and control your movement. If this occurs, the probability of you utilizing your self-defense moves and tools is extremely slim. Exceptions can be made for individuals with special needs, where the front seat area is much easier for them to access. Use your discernment.

PRE-ATTACK

INDICATORS

Knowing how to predict an attack is equally as important as knowing how to defend yourself if you are attacked. Most criminals, without even knowing, display specific indicators immediately (within seconds) before they attack an individual. These are involuntary physiological "signs" that project from a criminal when they are in fight or flight mode. All of these indicators happen due to the body's response to an adrenaline dump, preparing the attacker for engagement in violence. It is imperative that you continuously monitor your dashcam, your rearview, and side mirrors while driving. In the beginning, it will feel a little overwhelming but eventually, it will become second nature.

Below you will find a few pre-attack indicators to look for:

This is a brief introduction into the art of reading body language. I must elucidate that these are just indicators and not scientific evidence, as the science of body language is not an exact science. Human beings are complicated, and their mannerisms are not always straight forward. To get a more accurate reading, you would have to include many different variables. Much of which was deliberately excluded from this guide due to the complexity and time to explain. But, by piecing together a few of the behavior mannerisms outlined below, you should have a general idea of your passenger's intentions, which will allow you to plan accordingly.

BLANK STARE

A passenger who is planning to attack you will sometimes have a blank stare, almost like they are looking through you and they will also have delayed responses to statements or questions asked. This indicates that the attacker is preparing their next move, so they may be slow to respond.

Criminals often do this when mentally shutting down and getting ready to go on an aggressive physical autopilot. Blink rates may also noticeably go way up or way down as their body preps for an attack.

FLARING OF NOSTRILS

Another very noticeable cue to look for is the flaring of the nostrils. If you are speaking with a passenger and notice that they are breathing rapidly and that their nostrils flare, that is a sign that they are anxious or stressed because they are preparing to attack within seconds. Nostrils automatically flare to allow for more oxygen intake.

I recommend that you start taking the necessary precautions immediately.

NECK ARTERIES AND VEINS

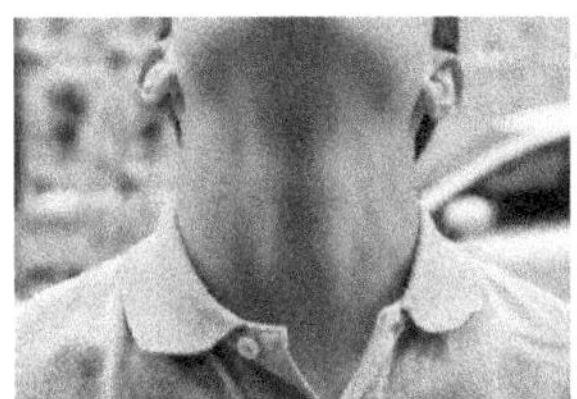

When someone is stressed, their pulse rate increases; while seasoned criminals have perfected the art of masking anxiety, our bodies are set on autopilot and can sometimes betray us by giving out involuntary cues. When your pulse rate increases, this can sometimes be visible in your neck arteries, and the veins in the forehead can also protrude.

If you're speaking with a passenger and notice any of the above, I would recommend that you immediately start looking for additional cues.

EYES

It is imperative to look for cues from a passenger's eyes. The eyes tend to give so much information. This information varies from person to person, but one very noticeable cue that almost every criminal has right before they attack is pupil dilation. The iris (the colored part of the eye) plays a vital role in the eye's proper functioning as its primary function is to control how much light enters the eye. Nerve impulses travel down the optic nerve after light enters the eye, affecting the pupil's size. It is very difficult for a criminal to control this as the pupil changes in size involuntarily.

When a criminal is about to attack, they experience extreme stress, anxiety, and fear (will they get a chance to execute their plan? or will they get caught?). In response to the rush of adrenaline in the body, their pupils will dilate.

DIRECTION OF THE GAZE

Use your mirrors or dashcam to observe the direction of your passenger's gaze as you speak to them.

Our brains are so beautifully made that each side of the brain controls the movement of the opposite side of our bodies (the left side of the brain controls movement on the right side of our body and the right side of the brain controls movement on the left side of our body). Neuroscience has revealed that the left side of the brain is our logical side. It deals with rational, linguistic activity and how we analyze things, while the right side of the brain deals with our creativity, imagination, and intuition.

Now that we know how the different sides of our brain function, it's a bit easier to determine the direction of the gaze and how it relates to intention.

If your passenger gazes to the right while answering your question, it's safe to assume that they are honest, but if they gaze to the left, they may be lying as they are tapping into their imagination and creativity.

Establishing the pattern for a passenger's eye direction will give you some indicator as to whether you need to be on a high or moderate alert while they are in your vehicle.

BLINK RATE

The blink rate of your passenger may also increase if they are planning to attack you. The increase in the blinking is due to the increase in cognitive activity in the brain because they are stressed.

It must be noted that increased blinking can also be a result of a medical condition or tiredness. So, you will have to look for additional cues.

RAISED EYEBROWS

When speaking with a passenger, focus on their eyebrows. Raised eyebrows signal discomfort. Three main emotions make eyebrows go up: surprise, worry, and fear. If you are talking to a passenger and they raise their eyebrows, and the topic isn't one that would logically cause surprise, worry, or fear, there is something else going on. Start taking necessary precautions.

TREMBLING

Another involuntary physical cue that an ill intent passenger may display immediately before attacking is trembling. This is as a result of the vast amounts of adrenaline coursing through their body before they strike. The trembling is usually noticeable in the hands or knees. It is important to note that this trembling may not necessarily be due to fear but rather a sign that the attacker is agitated and wants to strike as quickly as possible.

If you notice a passenger trembling, immediately get prepared to defend yourself if the need arises.

EXAGGERATED NODDING

Exaggerated nodding signals anxiety. When you're telling a passenger something, and they nod excessively, this may mean they are worried or stressed. Criminals are always looking for a sign that you are on to them, so it is crucial to look for the little things they do subconsciously. If you notice a passenger nodding extensively, it's essential to keep a poker face and not bring it to their attention. But, instead, use this information to start mentally planning how you will defend yourself.

BREATHING PATTERN

Observe your passenger's breathing pattern. If you notice a passenger panting, taking a big deep breath, or audibly sighing, these are all warning signs that should be taken seriously. The human body is well designed, so when adrenaline spikes, our breathing rate will increase. The passenger may be taking these actions to consciously slow their breathing rate and calm down so that they don't prematurely alert you to their plans.

It must be noted that the passenger may have an existing health condition. Ask if they are ok. If the passenger has no ill intent, they will be happy for your concern; however, if the passenger has ill intentions, your questions will quickly alert them that you are aware that something isn't right. They will immediately do one of two things, attack immediately or abandon their plan. Either way, I recommend that you prepare to defend yourself.

CLENCHED JAW

It's important to take a good look at your passengers' faces as they enter the car; this will be invaluable if the need ever arises for an investigation. Particular attention should be placed on the jaw area. If the passenger's jaw was relaxed when they initially entered the vehicle, and then you notice it suddenly clenches, for no apparent reason that you can see (not on their phone or tablet), this is something to take seriously, a this is an indication that the passenger may be preparing to attack.

I recommend that you immediately start mentally preparing how you will defend yourself.

SWEATING

If a passenger starts suddenly sweating profusely, especially around the forehead and cheeks, and the conditions don't warrant them to do so, I recommend that you begin to take the necessary precautions.

SUDDEN CHANGE IN STATUS

If you notice that a passenger is watching you and then suddenly looks away when you glance at them, it's safe to assume that they are probably trying to hide their intentions. (it could be that they find you attractive, but for safety reasons, assume the worst) I recommend that you be on high alert and immediately start paying special attention. It is crucial that you watch the passenger's every move.

It would be best if you prepared for a potential attack.

EMERGENGY

PROCEDURES

CARJACKING

AND OR ROBBERY

Taking into consideration that most of your passengers will probably be seated in the rear of the vehicle, it is logical to assume that if a passenger decides to attack you, they will most likely grab you by the neck and hold a weapon to your head or neck because this is the area of your body that they have access. If this happens, I recommend that you try your best not to panic, as this will make your brain seize up, and you will be incapable of higher thought.

You must remain calm, and then remain calm some more; the worst thing that you can do at this time is to agitate the attacker. Screaming, cursing, or having any form of outburst or movement may have dire consequences. Instead, reassure your attacker that you will be compliant. Remember, the attacker has leveraged control of your movement by having a weapon.

If you're going to make it out alive, you will need to use your logic, rationale, rhetoric, and persuasion; if you remain calm, all of these will be to your advantage.

If the attacker had intended to kill you, you would have already been dead, so every second and minute that passes during this encounter is a second or minute in your favor.

Maintain eye contact if you can, then calmly and preferably in the lowest pitch possible vocalize your actions before you do them, for example, "I am going into my pocket to get my wallet, or I am going into my bag to get my purse," and calmy hand it to them.

If what they wanted was your vehicle, calmly hand them the key and vocalize that you are opening the door and you are about to exit. Slowly open the door and get out.

The goal is to keep your attacker calm. I must repeat that it is crucial to continually reassure your attacker that you are not resisting and have no intention of fighting back. Remember, your attacker is probably nervous and anxious about the probability of being caught, so any sudden unnecessary movement or sound may trigger your attacker, and it might not end in your favor. So, it would be best if you remained calm because calm begets calm. If you are calm, your attacker will more likely be calm as well.

I do not recommend that you fight back at this stage; just give them what they ask for.

If robbery were their only intent, they will leave immediately once they get what they want.

You can, however, try your best to memorize anything you can about the attacker, for example, height, weight, clothing, smell, tattoo's, piercings, accent, hair color, race, ethnicity, just about anything that stood out to you as they walked to the car and while they were sitting in the vehicle.

Please make a note of the direction they went when they left.

This information could prove invaluable during an investigation.

KIDNAPPING

Your best chance of thwarting a kidnapping attempt is within the first minute; yes, that precious little window between 0-60 seconds could mean life or death. There is a rule of thought amongst security professionals which states that if you can dirtily and aggressively fight off your kidnapper within the first 20 seconds, you have a good chance of scaring them off. Forget about compliance; it's time to get aggressive. Do not be a soft target and never agree to be kidnapped.

Fight and fight hard. Do everything you can to get out of the car or not be pushed back into the vehicle. Keep your hands on the horn, set off the car alarm, blow your whistle or shrill alarm, use whatever self-defense tool that is within reach, poke the eyes, bend their fingers, bite them, kick the genitals, kick and scream as loud as you can. Make as much noise as you can. Courage can move mountains. Be bold and be brave; this is your window of opportunity; exploit it. If you unexpectedly and violently go wild and crazy within the first minute, you have a great chance of foiling the kidnapper's plan. I must repeat, do any and everything you can not to be taken.

If your kidnapper points a gun at you, he is doing this to intimidate you. His objective is to place you in a tactical disadvantage where you will comply in exchange for not being killed. Remember, if he intended to kill you, he would have done it already, so never give up and never give in. Still attempt to thwart the kidnapper's plan. If you're driving, stop the car and jump out immediately. If your parked, open the door and run. Position your body at an angle as you run; try not to turn your back to them as this makes you an easier target. Run, I mean run as fast as you possibly can and, in a zig-zag pattern. You may still be shot, but the chances of being shot in a vital area of your body is dramatically reduced if you run, and it's even better if you run in a zig-zag pattern and greater if you can change the zig-zag pattern as much as possible. The goal is to make your direction unpredictable. It is more difficult to shoot a target accurately if it's constantly moving.

If, for some reason, you cannot run fast or have some injury or disability, which may result in you being a slower runner, all is not lost; you can still run. It will be easier for you if you ran in a straight line away from the pointed gun in this particular case. However, you must turn your body at an angle (any angle) and try to duck and bend your upper body in different directions and positions as you run.

In both scenarios', the objective is to get away from the line of fire with as few injuries as you can. If there are objects, trees, or walls in the vicinity, try to bob and weave behind these objects while you run, as this will also help reduce the chances of you being hit.

However, if your initial resistance didn't work, you must immediately change your strategy from fighting physically to fighting mentally. Don't worry that your attempt to foil their plan will put you at greater risk; kidnappers expect resistance. You must remember at this point you are an object to them, and there is a reason that they kidnapped you, so they won't dwell too much on your resistance because all their effort will be placed on getting away and proceeding with their plan. Please do not panic and start believing it's the end; If you remain calm, you immediately gain a psychological advantage over your kidnapper. You're going to need to think and to think fast.

The intensity and duration of reactions tend to vary from person to person, which is understandable, given what has just occurred. Within the first couple of seconds, most individuals will experience shock, denial, confusion, disbelief, and fear. While these are common reactions to extremely stressful situations, you must try to maintain your composure as much as possible. As I mentioned previously, kidnappers are prepared and do expect resistance when they initially attempt to kidnap you, but once they have you in their possession, the entire scenario changes. Kidnappers are the most dangerous within the first 45 minutes, as this is the period where they are more prone to be stressed and will act impulsively. So, the quicker you regain your composure, the better you will be able to react sensibly.

If your kidnapper forces you to drive, never take them back to your home; not only will they know where you live and probably return, but you will also be putting your family and neighbors at risk.

Come up with some creative reasons to dissuade them from wanting to go to your home, such as security at the gate, or my neighbor is a police officer, or my house or neighborhood is under surveillance. Try just about anything that comes to mind to get them to change their plan.

If you were unable to get them to change their mind or they instruct you to drive to another location, intentionally crash your car into an object, structure or intersection. Choose an area where there are lots of people. Be mindful not to crash into individuals or animals.

Most kidnappers are smart and will probably assume that crashing your vehicle will be your next course of action, so I recommend that you remain calm and try not to bring it to their attention that you are looking for a possible location to crash. Keep your eyes on the road. You should know the area you are working in pretty well, so do a mental run-through of all possible places in your immediate vicinity where you can crash the vehicle. If they are threatening you with a weapon, you must catch them off guard to ensure that they don't try to hurt you

If the kidnapper overpowers you and pushes you into the passenger seat and drives, as soon as you see a populated area or your first opportunity, whichever comes first, jump out of the car. It is better to have bruises, scrapes, and a few broken bones than it is to be raped, tortured, and possibly murdered.

Try to jump out of the vehicle at an angle in the opposite direction the car is moving. Remember, your body will be moving at the same speed and direction as the vehicle, so in order not to be run over by the car you're in, you need to jump in the opposite direction. Be mindful of cars beside and behind; if possible, try to jump towards the side of the road where there is grass or dirt.   Tuck your body into a ball. Rest your chin on your chest and bring your arms and legs in as close as you can to your body and cover your head as much as possible.

I recommend that you plan your jump when the car slows down a bit. The slower the speed, the fewer injuries you will incur.

Try to hit the ground with your shoulder, as this will protect your head. It will also allow you to roll away from incoming traffic. You can survive with a broken collar or shoulder; you may not with a cracked skull, so protecting your head should be your main priority.

If they place you in the trunk, remain calm and think of ways of escaping. For a 10x 15 ft room, for a total gas volume of 1200 cu ft (34,000cu liters) at 1 atm (atmospheric pressure), the average healthy adult human has a respiratory minute volume of 6L/min. So, it would take $34000/6 = 5667$ mins, roughly about four days, to breathe in all the air volume of that size room. The trunk of a car is much smaller. All trunks have different sizes; however, it is estimated that the average size of a sedan's trunk ranges from 16-18 cubic feet, so if you use the same formula, it should take about 12 hours for a healthy adult human to breathe in the total air volume in a trunk of that size and about 9-11 hrs. for that person to suffocate due to the toxicity from carbon dioxide, so to ensure you have the maximum amount of time at your disposal it is important not to hyperventilate, breath regularly, and try not to panic; because if you do, this will increase the carbon dioxide (co2) content of the air and you will use up well-needed oxygen, which in reality will shorten your hours. Some vehicles have back seats that fold down; try to pry it open a bit, do this slowly and as quietly as possible. You do not want to draw the

kidnapper's attention. Prying the seats open will
increase ventilation, and you will also hear what
is being said.

Immediately look for the trunk release leaver and jump out as quickly as possible. Avoid jumping if the car is speeding or on a highway.

I recommend that you wait until the vehicle has slowed down enough where it is somewhat safe for you to jump. Traffic lights and stops signs are perfect opportunities. If they turn into a residential neighborhood, a lane, alley, or path, jump out immediately.

Do not jump when the car has reached its destination. This will enrage the kidnappers and may result in you being severely beaten, drugged, or immediately killed.

If your car has no leaver, try using whatever metal object you can find in the trunk to push on the center of the trunk near the latch, hopefully breaking it so that it opens. You can also try using the object to push out the taillights, where you can stick your hands out and signal to drivers behind and beside you for help. They may not stop to help you physically but will most likely call the police on your behalf.

You must try to time this activity to coincide when the car is driving fast, or there is lots of noise around. The last thing you want is for the kidnapper to drug, gag, or tie you up.

If you cannot push the taillights out, try pulling on the light's wires and cables to disconnect it. This might get the police's attention, and they will probably attempt to pull the car over for a faulty brake or taillight. If this happens the second, you hear the police officer's voice scream and kick the trunk to create noise.

If you cannot crash the vehicle or escape for some reason, it is imperative that you remain calm and come up with a plan C. If plan C doesn't work, remember you have 23 other letters in the alphabet. Never give up!

Your kidnapper is probably taking you to another crime scene. It would be best if you kept your eyes, ears, and nostrils open. As I mentioned previously, you should know the area you're working in very well. Try to figure out where they are taking you. If you are blindfolded, you will need to rely on your senses to decipher the direction the vehicle is traveling. Hopefully, you can remember what time it was when you were kidnapped, as this will help you estimate the direction you are heading. The heat on your face and hands from the sun may give you a hint as to the direction the vehicle is traveling. Feel for the position where the sun rests on your body; if the sun is directly overhead, that means its noon (the sun moves straight south at noon, moving east to west by 15 degrees every hour).

If you are in the Northern hemisphere, i.e., USA, Caribbean UK, Europe, Mexico, India, China, Japan, Some South American and Some African Countries, if you feel the sun rays facing you, that means you are heading South. If you feel the rays on the back of your head or neck, that means you are heading North. It will be the opposite if you are in the Southern hemisphere.

If the windows are down, you can also use the wind's direction to estimate the vehicle's direction. If it is possible and safe to do so, place your finger in your mouth to get it wet. (you can cough or sneeze to not bring attention), now, take your finger out; the side of your finger that gets cool is the direction that the wind is blowing from. If you are unsure if it's east or west, point your left hand in the direction where you feel the sun rays. If it feels as if the sun is directly shining on your hand, you're heading east, and the opposite direction is west.

These are all estimates, and your calculations may be a bit off. But by using these tactics, you should at least have a general idea of where they may be taking you.

If you were kidnapped at night and blindfolded, or the kidnappers locked you in the trunk, using the sun and wind will be absolutely out of the question. You could, however, count the number of turns, the length of time between the turns, and the sound the engine is making. Open your nostrils so you can identify familiar smells, make a note of any particular food, restaurant, market, bakery, or factory that you pass along the way. Listen for all sounds, voices, and conversations from pediatricians, note the accents, and try to decipher the individuals' age and sexes. Is there a lot of horns honking, or does it sound like there is lots of traffic? Do you hear the sound of the engines of a train or buses or trucks? Are there birds chirping or dogs barking? Do you hear children playing? Do you hear church bells or any other religious ceremony or prayer? Do you hear grocery carts moving? Do you hear the water from a fountain or waves crashing from the ocean or sea? Do you hear the vehicles' echo, or are your ears popping from the pressure as if you are in a tunnel, or do you feel and hear the car moving over grooves like crossing a bridge? Is the surface of the road smooth or bumpy? All of these clues will give you an idea as to the neighborhood or area they are taking you to. If you need to escape or call for help, knowing where you are will assist both yourself and the authorities.

MAKING IT OUT
ALIVE

As a rideshare driver, you were probably kidnapped for one of three reasons:

i. the kidnapper wants to use you for ransom, or,
ii. the kidnapper is a sexual predator or serial killer, or,
iii. they are planning to use your vehicle to commit a crime, and they didn't want you to go to the authorities before they had a chance to execute their plan.

However, you may not know the exact motive as to why you were kidnapped but try not to focus on that at this particular time as the first 24 hours of a kidnapping is the most crucial for your survival. All your attention should be placed at this present moment on making it out alive.
You may be placed in a temporary holding area before being taken to a more permanent location, they may also move you several times in the

process. If you're going to escape, try to do it while you're at the temporary location, preferably the first temporary location, as it will be a lot easier than if they moved you again. Temporary locations tend to be less secure and are usually more centrally located. The probability of you knowing where you are is high. Remember, the more often your moved, the harder it is for you to know where you are, and it's also more difficult for the authorities to find you.

If you are being held outside, identify the path that the kidnappers use to come and go.

Be observant and make a mental note of every detail of the room or area. Listen and try to identify any sound or activity inside and outside the building or area you are held captive. This will allow you to have an idea of the building or area's layout, like climbing stairs, water pipes for bathrooms, faucets in the kitchen, fridge door closing, washer and dryer, lawnmower, crushing of leaves or small branches as they walk, water flowing from a river/stream/canal or crashing from the sea/ocean, animal noises, traffic, etc. If you are being held in a tunnel or cave, you will hear an echo when there is movement.

Watch your kidnappers coming and going carefully and look for all doors and openings that could potentially lead to the outside and what are the potential obstacles, if any. Look for the direction they turn as they exit the area. Are your kidnappers armed? Are they volatile? Study your kidnapper's behavior patterns and schedule, look for any loophole, weakness, or vulnerability you can use to your advantage. It's time also to open your nostrils again and distinguish all smells. Count the number of kidnappers and make a note of their accents and physical characteristics. Try to look if they have any unique markings, features, or habits. If your kidnappers are speaking amongst themselves, listen keenly for names, and rank structure. The more information you have, the better you can plan and the greater your chances of escaping successfully.

This information will also be priceless to investigators if you are released, rescued, or you get an opportunity to escape.

Keep track of the time. If they have locked you away, you can make a note of the changes in temperature and the sounds from outside (birds or traffic) to differentiate between night and daytime. Timing is key if you are going to plan your escape. It will also allow you to know how long you have been held captive.

It is essential that you play brain games to keep your mind sharp, and this will also help you to remain calm, for example, rhyming, riddles, brain yoga, matching a song to the artist, memorizing plots of a movie, a color to flower, a city to a country, passages from books you've read, etc.

Stretching and flexing your hands and feet will also keep your muscles toned.

Eat whatever food they give you; it doesn't matter if you have no appetite or aren't hungry; force yourself to eat. You need your mental and physical strength so that you are prepared to jump on the first available opportunity to escape.

This will be very difficult to do, considering your present circumstances, but you must try your best not to let a sense of hopelessness creep in. If you believe in a higher power, now is the time to cling to that belief. If not, hold on to something meaningful to you, like your family, friends, pets, or an ideal. This will not only build your faith and give you something to live and fight for, but it will also offer relief from frustration, worry, and anxiety.

Try to remember all the stories of people who have overcome adversities against all odds; really, pick your brain for all reports you read or watched on the television or from situations or people you know personally. This will help to keep your hope alive, that you will make it out.

Set a particular private goal for yourself; for example, I need to be alive for this specific date, such as an event, anniversary, birthday, a family member's graduation, etc.

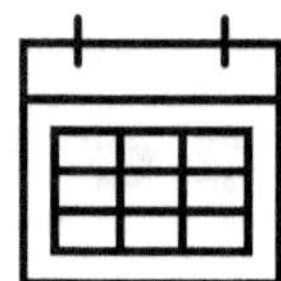

If you are still held captive past that date, set a new date. Remember, the longer you are alive, the better your chances of being released or rescued. This simple task will renew your hope minute by minute, hour by hour, or day by day.

If there are any other kidnapped victims in your vicinity, try to find some way of communicating with them. Remember, there is strength in numbers.

At this point, the kidnapper will probably tie up your hands and feet. Studies have shown that victims who are hostile and who present themselves in a threatening manner, especially during this stage, are the ones most likely to be killed. So, be humble, remain calm and follow all instructions. This period is very fragile, and you must, I repeat you must appear completely compliant because the slightest thing may antagonize the kidnapper, and the results may be catastrophic. You also don't want your kidnapper to think you need extra restraints. If you're going to escape having none or the least number of restraints is extremely important. Keep your head down and avoid making eye contact, as this may be regarded as challenging the kidnapper's domination. If the kidnappers think you won't fight back, they won't be as vigilant, and you can quickly capitalize on any holes that you find their security.

Now is the time to try to figure out why you were kidnapped. This will determine the risk you should take in attempting your escape. If you were kidnapped for ransom, your probability of survival is high as you are more valuable to your kidnapper alive than dead. However, if you were kidnapped by a serial killer or a sexual predator, your life is in imminent and immediate danger. You need to be vigilant and pay close attention to any signs that the kidnappers plan to kill you. If your kidnapper's demeanor suddenly changes, where they start acting frantic and desperate, and if they reveal their identity after concealing it initially, they are probably planning to kill you within the next 30 mins. You must attempt to escape immediately; even if you think the chance of success is not your favor, you still have a 50/50 chance of making it out alive. That's 50 more than if you didn't even try.

Make sure to offer your hands with the inside of your wrist pressed together. This position looks relatively harmless, but it's the best position to escape if you are tied up with duct tape or zip ties.

Duct Tape

It will take a lot of pressure on your part, and it will be painful, but as soon as the coast is clear, hold your hands above your head, as high as you possibly can, and force them down over your stomach passing your ribcage. Try to do this quickly and with as much strength and force as you can garner. Remember a sharp, quick pull with lots of force. The pressure should tear the duct tape. You can repeat the process if it doesn't work the first time.

If your hands are tied behind your back, this will be more difficult. Try to find any object with a sharp edge or a corner such as a; tabletop, door handle, corner of a wall or concrete/brick step, chair, countertop, stone/brick, sturdy shoe heel (you will need to get on your knees). Position yourself where the tape rests against the edge of the object and move your body up and down or side to side to try to cut through the tape. Be patient, and don't get frustrated; it may take time, but keep going until it breaks free.

Once your hands are free, now try to free your legs. Clasp your hands together and shove them quickly and forcefully into the tape. This should force your legs apart, bursting the tape. This process will hurt, and it will take a lot of effort, but remember your fighting for your life, so be committed to the fight and fight hard.

Zip Tie

Use your teeth to turn the zip tie's lock so that it is facing you and your wrists and palms meet. Make a fist with your hands, do this several times until you feel a slight ease in pressure, indicating that the ties have loosened. Now try to get your thumb out, as this will be the finger that will be easier to get out. But if you can get any other finger out first, that's ok. Once one finger is out, freeing yourself will be easy.

If your hands are tied behind your back, use the same method as you did for the duct tape.

Now try freeing your legs. Stand and bring your heels together so that your feet make a (V) shape. Immediately, squat down; you must do this forcefully, almost like you have a 300-pound barbell on your shoulders. As your bottom touches your heels, the zip tie should burst open. Repeat the process if it doesn't work the first time. This will be extremely painful, and you may be severely bruised; even though you will be in excruciating pain, try your best not to focus on the pain. All your attention should be placed on escaping. Remember a quick, forceful squat.

HUMANIZE YOURSELF

If you can't find any available opportunity to attempt your escape immediately, you must now try to humanize yourself to your kidnapper. Hopefully, this will buy you more time to either attempt your escape or be rescued or, if you're lucky, released.

This is basic psychology. If you can make them realize that you are human with blood running through your veins, in simple terms, view you as a real person, it might make one of your kidnappers more inclined not to kill you. All you need is one that will beg and convince the rest not to pull the trigger.

A great way to humanize yourself is to use your bodily functions Fart, urinate, defecate, burp. Yes, try to fart or burp as loudly as you can or make groaning sounds as you defecate. It may sound odd or ridiculous, but it will make you look more human to your kidnappers, and yes, they may laugh, but if that happens, it's a good thing. It shows your breaking down their defenses. Every minute that you are alive is a minute in your favor.

Other ways of humanizing yourself to the kidnappers:

- o Ask for small favors, like a drink of water or food, medicine, a book or magazine.

- o Talk to your kidnapper. Talk about any and everything, for example, family, sports, school, work, TV shows, whatever comes to mind. Hopefully, you will find a topic that is of interest to them. However, I recommend that you avoid politics and other sensitive issues, and please don't give any information about your or your family's finances.

o   Study your kidnappers and learn what behaviors you think will win their respect. Use this information to your advantage whenever dealing with them. If you can somehow manage to gain their respect, even ever so slightly, they may think twice about killing you.

o   Be as empathetic as you can. Try to build a relationship with your kidnapper while being observant and alert for any available opportunity to escape.

o   Inject humor into conversations. I do not recommend that you try to do this at the beginning or while your being moved from location to location as your kidnappers may be stressed and irritable at that time. They will also be wanting to instill fear so that you will be more compliant. However, when you think that they have moved you somewhere more permanent and you realize that some routine has been established, humor may help in the building of a relationship with your kidnappers.

Whichever tactic you choose to utilize in humanizing yourself is entirely up to you. Analyze your kidnapper and go with your gut.

But there is one thing that you don't have a choice in and that is the importance of remaining calm. No matter what you are enduring and or being threatened with, you must try not to freak out and start crying and screaming; this will make you appear too submissive. Maintain your composure and dignity as much as you can, and it is also equally as important not to act overly tough either as this will send a message that you are rebelling against your kidnapper. It's a balancing act. It sounds odd, and under the circumstances, it seems like a lot, but it's crucial for your survival.

Several serial killers have released victims because they did or said something that struck a chord.

Victim, 17-year-old Lisa Noland, who was kidnapped on her way home, managed to have talked her way out of being killed by serial killer Bobby Joe Long. Despite being raped and beaten for 26 hours, Noland wouldn't stop talking; she made her kidnapper think she liked him, and she enjoyed being raped by him. She gained his trust, and he dropped her home as if nothing had happened, thinking she was his new girlfriend.

In 1991 Tracy Edwards escaped Jeffery Dahmer's clutches by playing along and talking  to him; he kept him talking and talking until he got a chance to catch him off guard and punched him in the face; he then ran and jumped through the window. Police later found 17 dismembered bodies scattered throughout Jeffery Dahmer's apartment.

Serial killer Edmund Kemper revealed in an interview that he released one of his victims because she saw a pill bottle in his car and told him that her father has the same medication. 

That comment struck a nerve, and he pushed her out of his vehicle.

My point is, there is no hard and fast rule, do whatever it takes to stall, humanize, and or escape a kidnapper's clutches.

Be calm, be patient, and look for all and every opportunity to escape successfully. Remember, if your kidnapper wanted you dead, they would have killed you within the first 60 mins—your chances of survival increase with time.

MEDICAL ATTENTION

If you happen to escape, or your kidnappers decide to release you, try to find a neighbor or someone driving by who can contact the authorities on your behalf. Immediately seek medical attention, especially if you were raped and or beaten.

Your clothing and body will contain DNA that investigators can collect, which will later be used as evidence. This is also extremely valuable 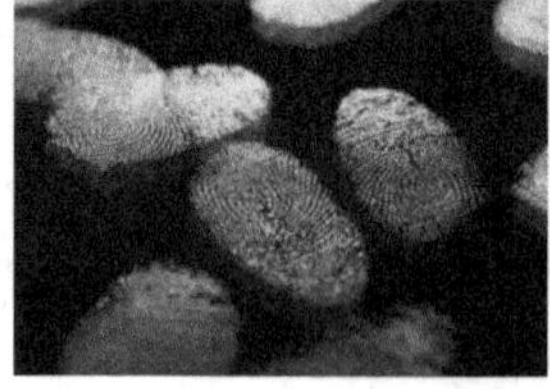 information for forensic experts. They can use the DNA samples taken to create a DNA profile.

This profile could potentially link and or incriminate your kidnappers. So, it is extremely important that you contact the authorities immediately.

If you were sexually assaulted, it is crucial that you inform the authorities and medical staff. The medical team will conduct a sexual assault examination. If this examination is done within 120 hrs. of the assault, the medical team can provide medications for certain sexually transmitted diseases (STDs) in the event you were exposed to any STDs during the assault. It must be noted that these medications are not 100% effective in preventing STDs, but they do, however, drastically lower the chances of the infection taking hold in your body.

I must repeat, it is imperative that you contact the authorities immediately after you escape or have been

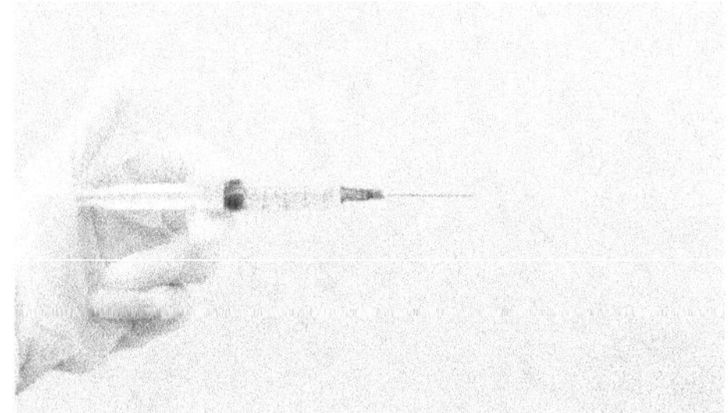

released

THE RESCUE

If you're lucky to have survived for an extended period, there is a pretty good chance that the authorities will attempt to rescue you. This is the second most dangerous ordeal, other than the initial kidnapping. More victims are often killed during rescue attempts than by torture or execution while held captive. Your kidnappers may become enraged by the rescue attempt and suddenly decide to kill you, or they may use you

as a human shield if the rescue team is shooting at them.

If you can, the second you hear, the rescue team immediately create distance between yourself and your kidnappers, try to find a corner to hide, and, if it's possible, barricade yourself. Your kidnappers will be preoccupied with defending themselves and won't have too much time to fight you.

Immediately drop to the ground or floor, remain still, either cover your head or cross your hands on your chest and bow your head, it depends on the position and space you are in, do not make any sudden moves, and follow all instructions. You do not want to get injured in the crossfire. Only move when the authorities advise you that it is safe to do so.

Give the authorities all the information that you can remember. If any of the kidnappers escaped or were not there at the time of the rescue: this information will be very beneficial to investigators.

ADDITIONAL INFORMATION

- Do not wear expensive jewelry, watches, or clothes. You are drawing attention to yourself.

- Be extra careful if working between 6 pm and 6 am, especially the hours between 12 am and 4 am, as most assaults, robberies, and murders of rideshare drivers occur during these hours.

- Be suspicious of passengers who give vague instructions. Insist on an exact address.

- Never be overly aggressive. Passengers are sometimes very difficult and rude, but you must try to remain calm and controlled. If you are too argumentative, the situation may escalate and result in a violent confrontation.

SUMMARY

Defending yourself as a rideshare driver is a combination of your mental approach, physical skills, the psychological skills you employ, and the verbal and body language you display.

I tried to cover all areas briefly.

While no-one wants to be the victim of an attack or kidnapping, the reality is it does happen. Unfortunately, the taxi/ rideshare industry continues to face disproportionately dangerous working environments, where thousands of drivers worldwide are assaulted, kidnapped, and or murdered each year.

You can read every book and collect all the available information; it means nothing if you don't use it. So, ask yourself: Are you willing to do whatever it takes to defend yourself and make it out alive?

Each time you turn on your rideshare driver availability, you need to permit yourself to do whatever it takes to make it out alive. If this isn't reconciled within you, your survival will be in jeopardy. There is no hard-fast rule when it comes to defending yourself. Assume the worst and tap into your inner core to find the courage that lays dormant inside. Be strong and face your fears head-on. If plan A doesn't work, move

immediately to plan B, then C, then D, etc. Don't think in terms of failure; instead, exhaust every potential possibility and exploit every available opportunity and please, without hesitation, take that chance if it becomes available.

It just might be your only chance to make it out alive.

Never Ever Give Up!

I hope you found the information provided helpful.

A short review will be greatly appreciated

Thank you!